Cooking Stetson Style:

Recipes and Photography

by Janet Beshara Stetson

RoseDog Books
585 Alpha Drive
Suite 103
Pittsburgh, PA 15238
Visit our website at *www.rosedogbookstore.com*

ISBN: 978-1-6386-7842-7
eISBN: 978-1-6386-7787-1

Cover Photo: Ceiling at the Uffizi, Florence, Italy

RoseDog🐾Books
PITTSBURGH, PENNSYLVANIA 15238

Sun filtered through windows: Sangrada Familia,
Barcelona, Spain

Dedicated to Barrett,
my wonderful husband of 40+ years,
who has always appreciated my cooking.

Sculpture, Montreux, Switzerland

CONTENTS

Skylight at the Galleria La Fayette, Paris, France

START THE DAY

Overnight French Toast

Buttered baking dish or rimmed cookie sheet big enough to hold the bread slices and deep enough to hold the liquid.

1 loaf of day-old French bread
6 eggs
1 ¼ C. milk
¼ C. half-and-half
¼ C. sugar
1 tsp. cinnamon (optional)
2 Tbsp. maple syrup
1 ½ tsp. vanilla extract
¼ tsp. salt

Slice the bread into ¾-inch slices. Arrange slices in baking dish. Pieces can be touching. In a large bowl combine all remaining ingredients. Pour over bread. Cover and refrigerate overnight. Turn slices over occasionally to make sure they are completely moist.

Bake in a 400° oven for 15 minutes. Turn pieces over and cook for another 15 minutes or until brown. Can be put under the broiler to get a nice, crispy finish.

Dust with powdered sugar.

Serve with fresh fruit or maple syrup.

Cinnamon Coffee Cake

Bundt pan

½ C. butter

1 C. granulated sugar

2 eggs

2 C. all-purpose flour

1 tsp. baking soda

1 tsp. baking powder

1 C. sour cream

½ tsp. vanilla

Topping:

½ C. brown sugar

¼ C. granulated sugar

½ tsp. cinnamon

½ C. pecans

Grease and flour Bundt pan. Cream butter and sugar with an electric beater until smooth. Add eggs and beat until color lightens. Sift together flour, baking soda, baking powder and salt. Add flour mixture to batter, alternating with sour cream. Add vanilla and beat for 1 minute or until thoroughly blended. Pour half the batter into the Bundt pan followed by half the nut mixture. Pour in the second half of the batter and top with the remaining nut mixture. Bake in a 350° oven for 40 minutes or until toothpick comes out clean. Let cool and invert onto serving plate.

Popovers

Typically, this is a recipe made to go with roast beef. But popovers will go with salad lunch or whenever rolls are recommended.

Muffin tin sprayed with Spam for easy clean-up.

Drippings from roast beef or cooking oil
3 eggs
1 ¼ C. milk
1 ¼ C. white flour
¼ tsp. salt

Heat the oven to 450°. Pour a shallow layer of beef drippings or cooking oil (not olive oil) on the bottom of each muffin tin. Put the pan in the oven to heat the oil before you pour in the batter. Remove the muffin tin from the oven. While the tin is heating assemble ingredients.

Put all ingredients in a large bowl and using a whisk, mix thoroughly. Do not over mix. Half fill muffin tins with batter. Put them in the oven and bake for 15 minutes or until golden brown. Remove popovers from the muffin tin and serve.

Serves 6.

One time I didn't have a standard-size muffin tin. I had to make the popovers in mini-muffin tins. Worked great!

Eggs in booth at a market in Lucerne, Switzerland.

Appetizers
Soups
Salads
Sauces

Architecture relief, Barcelona, Spain

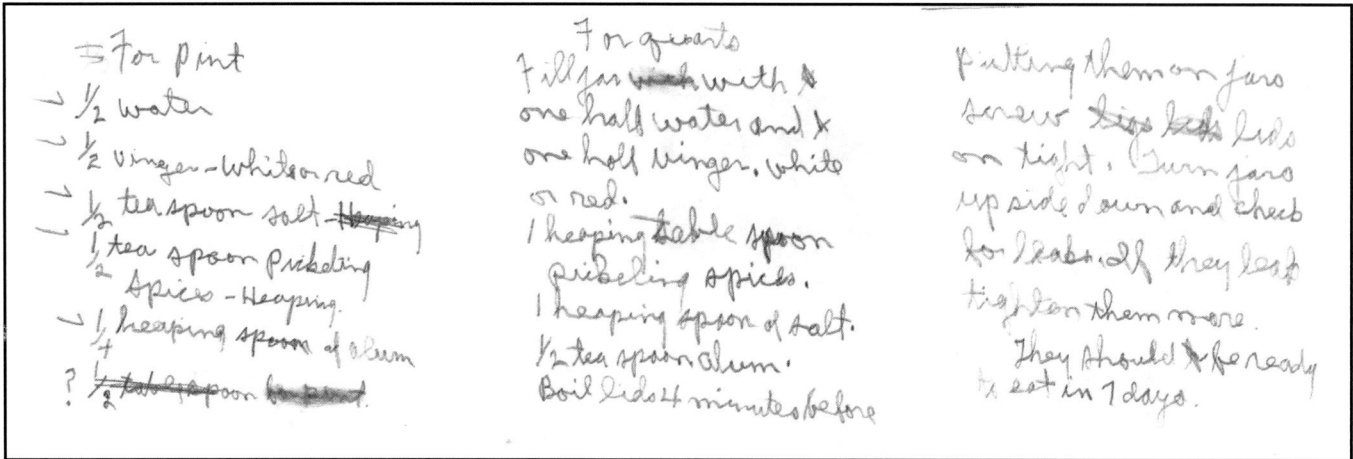

Papa's handwritten instructions

= For pint
→ 1/2 water
→ 1/2 vinger - White or red
→ 1/2 tea spoon salt ~~Heaping~~
→ 1/2 tea spoon pickeling
Spices - Heaping.
→ 1/4 heaping spoon of alum
? ~~1/2 table spoon~~

For quarts
Fill jar ~~with~~ with
one half water and
one half vinger, white
or red.
1 heaping table spoon
pickeling spices.
1 heaping spoon of salt.
1/2 tea spoon alum.
Boil lids 4 minutes before

Putting them on jars
screw ~~lids~~ lids
on tight. Turn jars
up side down and check
for leaks. If they leak
tighten them more.
They should be ready
to eat in 7 days.

Papadea's Sour Pickles

Assemble 4 one-quart canning jars, new lids and rings.
10 to 12 pickling cucumbers
Water
Vinegar
½ tsp. pickling salt
½ tsp. pickling spice
¼ heaping Tbsp. alum

Divide among the jars 10 to 12 pickling cucumbers. Cucumbers should be snug. Fill each jar with ½ water, ½ white vinegar. Add salt, spice, and alum to each jar.

Fill a small saucepan with water. Bring to a boil. Boil 4 new lids for 4 minutes. Using jar rings put lids in place and screw down firmly. Turn each jar upside down to test for leaks. If liquid escapes, tighten more. Pickles should be ready to eat in 7 days.

If you want dill pickles, just add 6 sprigs of fresh dill or 1 Tbsp. dried dill to each jar.

Refrigerator Bread n' Butter Pickles

8 small pickling cucumbers, unpeeled and cut into ¼-inch-thick medallions

1 medium onion, cut in half and thinly sliced

1 C. cider vinegar

3/4 C. sugar

4 ½ tsp. kosher salt

2 tsp. mustard seed

½ tsp. dry mustard

½ tsp. turmeric

½ tsp. crushed red pepper flakes (optional)

½ tsp. celery seed

Combine vinegar, sugar, salt, mustard seed, dry mustard, turmeric, crushed red pepper, and celery seed in a saucepan. Heat to boiling over high heat, stirring occasionally. Boil 1 minute.

Put cucumbers and onions in a container with a tight-fitting lid such as a plastic storage bin. Pour liquid over cucumbers and onions. Cool to room temperature, stirring occasionally. Cover and chill overnight. After pickles are ready, you can portion out pickles and liquid into smaller jars and cover each with a tight-fitting lid.

LEBANESE PICKLED TURNIPS

In 2 one-quart jars divide equally:

1 lb. turnips (about 5 or 6)

1 small beet

4-5 sprigs celery leaf, or ½ tsp. celery seed

2 C. water

1 C. white vinegar

2 tsp. Kosher salt

3 to 5 cloves garlic, minced

Peel turnips and beet. Slice into 1/8th-inch half-moons. Pack the turnips, beets, garlic and celery into sanitized quart jar, layering the ingredients. Meanwhile, combine the water, vinegar, salt in a saucepan and bring to a simmer. Pour the hot brine over the vegetables, completely covering them. Set aside to cool, then screw on lids, label, date and refrigerate. Wait 3-5 days before eating. They will keep in the fridge for up to 1 month.

Pickling Basics

Kosher or pickling salt is salt that does not have iodine in it. Iodine would make the pickles soft.

Pickling cucumbers are generally small. More importantly than that, they are not waxed. Waxed cucumbers would not allow the brine to penetrate the rind.

Jars and rings can be reused. Lids, though, need to be new so there is an airtight seal.

Ceiling in Gaudi "Casa Batllo," Barcelona, Spain

Tahini
Serve all of the dishes below with pita bread

Tahini can be purchased from the local import store in a jar or a can. When purchased, the tahini in the container will have separated with the oil rising to the top. In order to make the tahini usable it has to be homogenized.

Do this by emptying the entire container into the bowl of a food processor. Whirl paste until it is thoroughly mixed. Return the paste into the original jar. Use the raw tahini as required by each individual recipe. Unused Tahini will return to separated state. For future use, repeat mixing the paste before use. Also, unused tahini can keep indefinitely in your pantry.

Hummus Tahini

1 can chickpeas or garbanzo beans
1 recipe Tahini Sauce

Drain chickpeas, retaining the water in case you have to use to adjust consistency of the dip. Put all ingredients in the container of a food processor and beat the desired consistency. Adjust seasoning to taste.

Tahini Sauce

1 clove garlic, minced
½ tsp. salt
½ C. tahini
½ C. lemon juice
Water

In your food processor container add tahini, lemon juice, salt and garlic.
With the processor running, pour water into the mixture until the desired consistency.

Baba Ghannouj
(Eggplant and Tahini Dip)

1 medium eggplant
1 recipe of Tahini Sauce

Cut the eggplant in half. Slow roast the two halves over low heat on a grill, broiler or in a skillet. Turn over to roast all surfaces. Outsides might get toasty. That is fine. When the meat of the eggplant is soft, scoop out of the shell. Discard skin. Add 1 recipe of tahini and the eggplant to the container of a food processor. On pulse beat mixture to desired consistency. I like it chunkier more than pureed. Correct for flavor. May have to add salt, lemon, or garlic.

How to Grow Tomatoes

Tomatoes from my garden

Select tomato plants:

Purchase tomato plants from a local garden store. This ensures that you get plants that are suggested for your area. Plants should be placed 2 feet apart, so buy what will fit in the space that you have available. I purchase 2 of each variety that suits my preferences.

For instance, I like some that produce early fruit. I also like some that produce medium-size fruit, since there are just 2 of us and one tomato constitutes a "serving." You might go for big tomatoes or something more exotic, like heirlooms. The reason why you don't plant all the same variety is that some varieties may perform better than others in any given year, depending on the weather for that year, which is impossible to predict.

Timing:

Find out what the average last day of frost is for your region. Shoot for that day to do your planting. Of course, watch the weather report before you actually put the plants in the ground.

Prepare ground:

Tomatoes like new ground. If you use the same plot every year, purchase a 40 lb bag of manure and a 40 lb bag of topsoil for every 6 plants, and mix the soil in a wheelbarrow. Dig holes where you are going to put your plants and fill the holes with the soil mixture.

Purchase and Plant Tomatoes:

Buy tall plants. Before planting, strip all but the top 4" of leaves and plant as deep as possible in the new ground that you have provided. The reason for this is that the tomato plants will grow roots from the stem that is subterranean. This gives the plants access to the moisture deep underground during the hot summer.

Whatever method you use to tie up your plants (poles or cages) as they grow, situate them at the same time as your planting. This avoids disturbing the roots of the plants when they get older.

Plant your tomato plants in your prepared bed. As a last step, use a thin stick to stick in the ground right alongside of the plant. I use a wooden skewer, but any twig will do. This prevents "Cut Worms" from choking off the plant when it is young. As the plant matures and the stalk gets thicker, this is no longer an issue.

Gazpacho Soup
(Cold Tomato Soup)

2 ripe tomatoes, peeled

1 cucumber, peeled

¼ C. diced green pepper

¼ diced onion

4 leaves of sweet basil

1 C. canned tomato juice

2 Tbsp. cider vinegar

Salt and pepper

1 clove of garlic, minced

In order to peel tomatoes, cut the stem end off. Score the skin from top to bottom 4 times. In a small saucepan, bring water to a boil. Dip each tomato one at a time into the boiling water. Remove after one minute. Drain on a paper towel. When cool, peel skin off tomatoes.

Before proceeding slice 4 medallions of cucumber and reserve for garnish. Put all ingredients in a food processor. Pulse ingredients until desired consistency. I like mine with a few chunks for texture. Chill soup and serve in individual ramekins with a slice of cucumber floating on top. Serves 4.

Poppyseed Dressing

1½ C. sugar
2 tsp. dry mustard
2 tsp. salt
⅔ C. cider vinegar
3 Tbsp. onion juice (find at Walmart or online)
2 C. salad oil (not olive oil)
3 Tbsp. poppy seeds

Using a food processor mix sugar, mustard, salt, and vinegar. Add onion juice and stir in thoroughly. Add oil slowly, beating constantly, and continue to beat until thick. Add poppyseeds and beat for a few more minutes. Store in the refrigerator.

Poppyseed dressing is especially good on any kind of fruit. Try adding avocado too. Enjoy!

Door at Sangrata Familia, Barcelona Spain

Salata:
Lebanese Salad Dressing

2 tsp. salt

½ tsp. pepper

1 large button garlic

10 leaves fresh or 2 tsp. dry mint

3 leaves fresh sweet basil or ½ tsp dried

Juice of 2 lemons or ½ C. lemon juice

3/4 C. olive oil

Put all of the spices in a pestle and crush with a mortar until well blended. Place mixture in a jar and add lemon and olive oil. Shake well. Pour desired amount over salad. Refrigerate any unused dressing. Let stand at room temperature before serving.

Serves 4-6.

Napkin Art, Barge Cruise, France

TUNA SALAD WITH SALATA DRESSING

1 envelope plain tuna

½ apple, diced

1 tomato, diced

1 handful of potato chips, crushed

1 dill pickle spear, diced

Whole lettuce leaves for base

¼ C. Salata Dressing

1 tsp pickled ginger juice

¼ C. dried wasabi edamame, crushed

1 Tbsp. jalapeño, diced

1 Tbsp. soy sauce

Optional ingredients:

Scallions

Parsley

Mix together the Salata Dressing, edamame and soy sauce. Assemble the remaining ingredients and serve on top of lettuce leaves. Serves 2.

Pesto

3 C. packed fresh basil leaves

4 cloves garlic

¾ C. grated Parmesan cheese

½ C. olive oil

¼ C. pine nuts

½ C. chopped fresh parsley (optional)

Combine basil, garlic, Parmesan cheese, olive oil, and nuts in the bowl of a food processor or blender. Blend to a smooth paste. Add parsley if desired.

Pesto & Shrimp over Pasta

Just Slaw

1 head of cabbage

1 onion

½ C. sugar

1 tsp. celery seed

1 tsp. sugar

1 ½ tsp. salt

1 tsp. prepared Dijon mustard

1 C. cider vinegar

1 C. salad oil

Using the "slaw blade" on a food processor, cut up all of the cabbage. If a food processor is not available, cut cabbage into small strips. Stir in sugar. Slice onions into fine rings. Alternate three layers starting with the cabbage, then onions, and so on, ending with onions.

Combine celery seed, sugar, salt mustard and vinegar in a saucepan. Bring to a rolling boil. Stir with a small wire whisk. Add salad oil and return to a boil. Pour over slaw. DO NOT STIR. Cover and refrigerate several hours or overnight.

Mozzarella Balsamic Salad

Fresh Sweet Basil

Fresh Tomatoes

Avocado

Fresh Mozzarella

Fresh Figs

Salt

Pepper

Balsamic Vinegar

Place all ingredients on individual salad plates. Drizzle Balsamic Vinegar over all.

Produce Market in Barcelona, Spain

Staircase on the cruise ship

YOGURT

Any amount of milk. 1 gallon, 1 quart, 2 quarts. The amount depends on how much yogurt you want to end up with. Final amount will be slightly less than what you start out with.

¼ C. starter. This can be some of the yogurt from the previous batch or plain yogurt that you purchase at the store.

Choose a saucepan that is 2X as large as your quantity of milk. Spray the inside of the pot with Pam. This is not necessary for the making of the yogurt. It does, though, make clean-up easier.

Pour milk into saucepan. Over medium heat, bring milk to a rolling boil. This serves to neutralize the pasteurization. Pasteurized milk will not allow the yeast to grow for the formation of yogurt. Immediately remove the pot from the stove, careful not to let the milk boil over.

Let the milk cool to lukewarm. The temperature should be about 90 degrees. The old-fashioned method of testing the temperature is to insert your little finger in the milk. If the milk is cool enough for you to count to 10, then it is cool enough. This is obviously an inexact determination of when the milk is ready, but it works. The goal here is to not have the milk so warm as to kill the yeast in the starter. Cooler than 90 degrees is fine.

You can leave the milk in the pot and stir the yogurt starter into the milk. Use the pot lid to cover the saucepan. Wrap the whole pot in a blanket and set aside. Let sit overnight or for 8 hours.

Alternative method of storing the milk, is to pour the warm milk, which has had the starter mixed in, into a plastic a plastic storage bowl with a tight-fitting lid. I like this better because I can put it into the refrigerator after it has set overnight. Wrap the container in a blanket and set aside as described above.

When the yogurt has clambered, you can use cheesecloth to drain the extra whey (the liquid on the top). Line a bowl with large piece of cheesecloth. Pour the yogurt into the cheesecloth. Tie up the corners and hang on the faucet with a bowl underneath the cheesecloth. Let the whey drain for two hours or until it is the desired consistency. I like to use my yogurt as I would sour cream so that is the consistency that I prefer. Spoon the yogurt back into the storage container. At this stage, save ¼ cup for starter for your next batch. The starter can be frozen. Refrigerated, the yogurt will last a week or two. There are no preservatives, so if left too long the yogurt will get sour. Then you need to dispose of the batch.

To make "Lubbneh" (cheese the consistency of cream cheese) let the yogurt stay in the cheesecloth longer. This product can be used to substitute for cream cheese in recipes. It is more tart than cream cheese, so you will have to decide you like the difference when you use this as a substitute. I prefer the tartness of the lubbneh with salmon as opposed to cream cheese.

Tabouli

½ C. bulgur (cracked wheat)
2 bunches parsley
1 bunch scallions
2 large, solid tomatoes
½ C. fresh mint
Juice of 3 lemons
½ C. olive oil
1 Tbsp. salt
½ tsp. pepper

Place bulgur in a sieve. Place the sieve in a bowl and cover bulgur with water. Set aside. Use a mortal and a pestle to grind the mint, salt and pepper together. Place mixture in bottom of salad serving bowl. Squeeze lemons and add juice to bottom of bowl. Dice tomatoes and add to salad bowl. Do not untie parsley bunches. Wash by swishing heads in water. Then shake off water. With a large knife, cut off the major portion of the parsley leaves. Discard stems. Place parsley in salad spinner and spin off as much water as possible. Using food processor set on pulse, chop parsley leaves, being careful not to puree. Add to bowl. Cut scallions in ¼" pieces. Add to bowl. Bulgur should be swollen with the water it has absorbed. Take sieve out of water and let drain over the sink for 30 minutes. Add wheat to salad bowl. When all ingredients are in the salad bowl, pour olive oil over all. Stir. Refrigerate. Best if made several hours before serving to give the bulgur a chance to marinate.

Outdoor Market

ENTREES

Salata Dressing as a Marinade

Salata Dressing is a great marinade for:

- Any kind of fish
- Shrimp
- Flank Steak (score the steak on both sides so the marinade can penetrate the meat). Let marinade for 30 min. before grilling.
- Chicken

(The above meats can be grilled after marinating.)

Dressing can be used for:

- Tossed Salad
- Black-eyed peas, either served cold or hot
- Boiled new (red) potatoes either cold or hot. Great summertime potato salad since mayonnaise is not used.
- Any vegetable can be grilled after marinating in the Salata

Add extra ingredients to the above dishes. Suggestions are Scallions, Parsley, Pepper flakes, Red onions. Possibilities are only limited by your imagination.

Meat Mixture for Vegetables

1 lb. quality ground beef

½ C. white or Jasmine rice

½ tsp. cinnamon

1 ½ tsp. salt

¼ tsp. pepper

1 clove garlic, minced

16-oz. can diced tomatoes

1 C. tomato juice

Mix meat, rice, spices and tomatoes in a bowl. This is the filling that you will use for cabbage rolls, grape leaf rolls, and stuffed squash.

Grape Leaf Rolls

1 recipe of meat mixture

1 jar grape leaves from an import store

1 Tbsp. lemon juice

1 pint tomato juice

Unfurl grape leaves. Lay each grape leaf flat. Place 1 Tbsp. meat mixture on the leaf. Roll leaf around meat by tucking sides over the ends and roll the leaf cigar style. Put each roll in a pot arranging in layers. Weight with a china dish on top of the rolls to keep them from unfurling while cooking. Pour tomato juice in pot to cover rolls. Add lemon juice. Bring to a boil and simmer for one hour. Test to make sure the rice is cooked. Serve with yogurt.

STUFFED SQUASH

8 yellow squash or zucchini squash. Purchase the fattest ones you can find.
1 recipe meat mixture
4 or 5 extra cloves of garlic for the pot
1 qt. tomato juice
Large pot

Wash squash. Trim the neck of the squash down far enough to be able to get a small spoon inside the squash. Throw away the stem. Cut the neck pieces into medallions and place at the bottom of the pot. Core out seeds and some of the flesh from the center of the squash, making sure not to break through the outer shell. Once again, put the scrapings in the bottom of the pot.

Using your hands, stuff the meat mixture inside of the squash, squeezing as much liquid out in order to stuff as much as possible into the cavity. Repeat with all of the squash. As you fill them put the squash in the pot, setting them as close together as possible.

Add the garlic cloves to the pot. Place an inverted china plate on top of the squash to keep them from floating. Pour tomato juice over all to cover squash. Cover the pot with a lid and bring everything to a boil.
Set on simmer and cook until rice is cooked and squash is cooked. Serve with yogurt. Logically, fat squash will hold more meat mixture. Farmers markets sometimes have fat squash since they have less uniformity in their product.

I use a melon baller to scrape out the insides of the squash. You can use an apple corer also. If you have neither of those, go ahead and use a small spoon.

CABBAGE ROLLS

1 head of cabbage

1 recipe of meat mixture

4 or 5 extra cloves of garlic for the pot.

Wash cabbage and cut the core out.

Fill a large pot with water. Bring to a boil. Keep water at a slow boil.

Drop the cabbage into the boiling water. Cut leaves off the core one at a time and separate the leaves from the head gently, being careful not to tear the leaves. Remove each leaf from the pot to a tray when they are sufficiently wilted. Leaves should be pliable. After all the leaves are wilted, it is time to trim the ribs. Use a knife to trim the ridge of the rib so the leaves can be rolled. If leaves are large, they can be cut in half. Save leaf trimmings to line the bottom of the pot that you are going to put your rolls onto. Prepare a large pot for the cabbage rolls. In a large pot, line the bottom of the pot with the scraps from the cabbage leaf trimmings.

Lay flat each leaf on a flat surface. Place a spoonful of filling into each leaf. Roll leaf around filling and tuck in the sides as you roll the leaf. Amount of filling is determined by the size of the cabbage leaf. Use enough meat mixture so the cabbage leaf can be rolled around it overlapping the edges. Place in the pot, arranging the cabbage rolls snugly. As you are layering the rolls, add garlic cloves to the pot. When all of the rolls are put into the pot, put a china plate on top of the rolls to keep them from unrolling. Pour tomato juice in the pot enough to cover the rolls. Cover the pot and bring to a simmer on the stove. Let simmer for 1 hour or until rice is cooked. Serve with plain yogurt.

Stuffed Eggplant

1 lb. ground beef
2 eggplant
1 onion
2 tsp. salt
½ tsp. black pepper
Dash of cinnamon
¼ C. pine nuts
Olive oil
Plain yogurt (optional)

Brown ground meat and onion. Season with salt, pepper and cinnamon. When cooked, add pine nuts. Set aside.

Wash eggplant. Cut eggplant in half longways, leaving stem, peel and seeds intact. Pour olive oil in skillet and place skillet over medium heat. When hot, place eggplant pieces in skillet. Sear all sides of eggplant and cook until all sides are tender. Transfer eggplant halves to baking dish, skin side down. Cut slit down center of eggplant and gently separate halves without breaching the skin.

Spoon meat mixture into slit. Pour can of tomatoes over all. Add one inch of water to cover bottom of pan. Bake in oven at 350° for one hour or until eggplant is fully tender. Serve over rice. Top with yogurt. Serves 4.

Eggplant can also be softened by grilling. Place halves over grill and turn often to cook without charring.

Baked Kibbee (Lebanese Meatloaf)

Meat Mixture:

2 lbs. lean ground beef

1 onion

10 leaves mint or 1 Tbsp. dried mint

4 leaves sweet basil or 1 tsp. dried sweet basil

2 C. Burghul (cracked wheat), fine grain

Salt, pepper, a dash of cinnamon to taste

¼ C. butter, melted

Place Burghul in a mesh strainer and place the strainer in a bowl. Cover the Burghul with water. Let soak for 15 minutes. Lift the strainer out of the water and place over an empty bowl or sink and leave to drain. Drain while assembling the other ingredients.

Cut the onion into chunks and put into the bowl of a food processor. Chop fine. Add meat, mint, basil, and spices to the food processor bowl. Add drained Burghul and process until uniform. Meat mixture will look like pate'.

Filling:

1/2 lb. chopped beef

1 onion, chopped

¼ C. pine nuts

Salt, pepper, dash of cinnamon to taste

Sauté meat and onion in a skillet until meat is cooked. Add pine nuts and seasonings.

Assembly

In 12x8" pan, put ½ of the meat mixture. Using your hands, spread the meat mixture evenly on the bottom of the pan. Spread the filling evenly on top of the meat mixture. Cover with remaining meat by taking a handful of meat mixture and making patties. Lay the patties edge to edge on the top of the filling. Smooth surface and fill in gaps using small portions of the meat mixture to cover the top completely. Score by cutting the surface not all the way through, into 12 serving sizes. Score designs into each square. Crosshatch, V's, checkerboard are some suggestions. Pour melted butter on top. Bake at 325° for 30 min. or until edges brown and pull away from the sides of the pan. Makes 12 servings. Serve with plain yogurt.

Kibbee Nayee (Raw Kibbee)

Kibbee Nayee is merely the uncooked meat mixture. Mound the meat mixture on a platter and garnished with raw onions and parsley. Olive oil can be used as a little drizzle over all. Actually, much like how ceviche "cooks" fish with lime juice, the meat is "cooked" with the acid from the onion. Serve with pita bread.

How to Assemble Kibbee

Half of the Kibbee mixture on the bottom

Create patties to assemble top layer

*Fill gaps between patties
to cover the top completely*

Make squares by scoring design into top.

Scored squares in Kibbee pan

Make designs in each square

Lebanese Green Beans

½ onion, diced
1 lb. green beans
16-oz. can diced tomatoes
½ tsp. salt
¼ tsp. pepper
1/8 tsp. cinnamon
1 Tbsp. olive oil

Clean green beans. Cut the ends off and cut beans into preferred serving size. Put olive oil, onion and green beans into a microwave-proof lidded dish. Stir to coat the beans and onion. Cover dish and microwave for 5 minutes on high. Uncover dish and add all of the contents of the can of tomatoes. Add all of the spices. Recover and cook another 5 minutes or until the beans are the desired texture.

Bridge at White Rock Lake, Dallas, Texas

Chili n' Beans

2 lbs. ground beef

2 medium onions, diced

1 16-oz. can diced tomatoes

1 Tbsp. chili powder

1 tsp. cumin

1 large bay leaf

¼ tsp. ground cloves

½ tsp. paprika

½ tsp. cayenne pepper

1 clove garlic, minced

3 tsp. salt

¼ C. cider vinegar

2 10-oz. cans red kidney beans

In a heavy pot, brown the meat. Add the onions and green pepper. Cook until the onions are transparent. Add the tomatoes. Bring the mixture to a boil. Add all remaining ingredients except the beans. Let simmer 1 hour. Add the beans and cook until they are hot. Serve.

Janet's Spaghetti Sauce

1 lb. 90% ground beef

1 onion

1 16-oz. can tomato sauce

1 6-oz. can tomato paste

Use the paste can to measure one can of water. Add to pot

¼ C. fresh oregano

5 leaves sweet basil

2 buttons of garlic

1 Tbsp. salt

½ tsp. ground pepper

¼ C. quality red wine

Parmesan cheese

Dice onion. Put onion and ground beef in a 4-quart pot. Cook until the meat is brown. In a mortar place salt, pepper, oregano, sweet basil and garlic. Using a pestle grind all of the ingredients until the garlic and leaves are pulverized. Set aside. Put all of the tomato sauce and tomato paste and water in the pot. Add all of the spices. Cover and simmer for at least ½-hour. Pour the wine in and stir. Serve over fresh pasta. Sprinkle with parmesan.

Veal Piccata

½ C all-purpose flour

2 tsp. salt, divided

½ tsp. ground black pepper

4 pieces veal scallopini, about ¾ lb.

1 ½ Tbsp. vegetable oil

5 Tbsp. butter, divided

1 C. dry white wine

½ C. chicken stock

1 clove minced garlic

Juice of 1 lemon

2 Tbsp capers, drained

1 Tbsp. parsley leaves

In a shallow bowl combine the flour, 1 ½ tsp. salt, and pepper and stir to combine thoroughly. Quickly dredge the veal scallops in the seasoned flour mixture, shake to remove any excess flour.

Heat the oil in a large skillet over medium-high heat, hot but not smoking. Add 1 ½ Tbsp. of the butter and working quickly and in batches if necessary. Cook the veal until golden brown on both sides, about 1 minute per side. Transfer to a plate and set aside. Deglaze the pan with wine and bring to a boil, scraping to remove any brown bits from the bottom of the pan. When the wine is reduced by half, add the chicken stock, garlic, lemon juice and cook for 5 minutes or until the sauce has thickened slightly. Whisk in the remaining ½ tsp. salt, remaining butter and the chopped parsley. When the butter has melted, return the veal scallops to the pan and cook until heated through and the sauce has thickened, about 1 minute.

Iron Sculpture, Clark Gardens, Weatherford, Texas

How to Pan Dress a Fish

Purchase trout from the fishmonger that is whole, deboned and butterflied. Or, you can pan dress the trout yourself. It is important to have a very sharp boning knife.

Buy whole trout. If the fish hasn't been descaled, under running water rub the surface of the fish with a scrubbing pad until all of the scales have been removed. Next, cut the head off right after the gills. Grab the dorsal fin with fingers and cut around it to remove.

Small spine bones will come away with the fin. Slit the belly of the fish from the front end to the tail.

Flip the fish so its belly is facing upward. Separate the sides of the fish into a butterfly. Look for the fish bone structure running down the center of the fish.

Run your knife along each side of the spinal bone, cutting through the bones but not the outer skin. With fingers pull the spine away from the trout, cutting off at the tail, and discard. While the main bone structure is now removed, the fish will just have remaining bones in the soft flesh on either side.

Insert the knife and run it between the rib bones and the flesh. Cut the ribs away on both sides of the fish. There will be small bones remaining. You can remove with tweezers or remove after cooking.

Prepare the fish as desired.

Prince Albert Restaurant, Antibes, France

Pecan-Crusted Trout

½ C. dry bread or cornbread

2 Tbsp. pecans

½ tsp. salt

¼ tsp. garlic powder

¼ tsp. black pepper

½ C. buttermilk

½ tsp. red pepper flakes

3 Tbsp. all-purpose flour

4 Trout or Tilapia Filets

Vegetable oil

4 lemon wedges

Trout caught by Barry and me in Port Mansfield,

Combine first 6 ingredients in the container of a food processor and "pulse" until mixture is uniform and crumbly. Put breadcrumb mixture in a shallow bowl. Put buttermilk in a medium bowl. Put buttermilk in a medium bowl. Place flour in a shallow dish. Dredge each fillet in flour. Then dip in buttermilk mixture. Then dredge in breadcrumb mixture.

Coat the bottom of a large non-stick skillet with oil. When oil is heated to medium high, add 2 fillets. Cook uncovered 3 minutes on each side or until fish flakes easily when tested with a fork. Repeat procedure with remaining fillets. Serve with lemon wedges.

STUFFED TROUT*

4 whole pan-dressed fish
1/2 C. hearty bread cubes
¼ C. diced onion
16 fresh sweet basil leaves
Salt, pepper, garlic powder
Olive oil

Place diced onion in a sauté pan with some olive oil. Sauté onion until transparent. Toss in the bread cubes and stir. Set aside.

Lay each fish open on a baking sheet with the inside of the fish facing up. Sprinkle both sides of the fish with salt, pepper and garlic powder. Divide onion/bread mixture evenly between the four fish. Spread mixture on one side of the open fish. Distribute the basil leaves among the fish. Fold the fish halves together. Rub the outsides with olive oil. Place on Cookie Sheet.
Bake at 325° for 25 minutes.

Prepared fish can be grilled or sautéed. If you choose to grill, use a grill basket and flip to cook both sides. If you choose to sauté, cook each side until flaky.

*Recipe can be used for any whole fish. Another suggestion is Branzini (aka Mediterranean Sea Bass)

LINGUINE WITH SEAFOOD

4 Tbsp. unsalted butter, divided

1 bu. scallions, chopped

½ lb. medium shrimp, shelled and deveined

½ lb. sea scallops, sliced into medallions

1 clove garlic, minced

¼ C. chopped parsley

1 Tbsp. fresh basil

1 Tbsp. fresh oregano

4-oz. canned minced clams & juice

Juice of one lemon

½ C. dry white wine

Salt

Pepper

1 Tbsp. corn starch dissolved in 2 Tbsp. water

1 lb. linguine, cooked

1 Tbsp. sour cream

Melt 2 Tbsp. butter in a skillet over medium-high heat. When the foaming subsides, add scallions, shrimp, scallops, garlic and herbs. Stir until shrimp turns pink, about 2 min. Add clams, clam juice, lemon juice and wine. Season to taste with salt and pepper. When the liquid has returned to a boil, reduce heat and simmer 5 minutes. Stir in corn starch mixture. Cook a few minutes longer to thicken.

At the same time that you are making the sauce, cook pasta. Drain and place in a serving bowl. Stir in 1 Tbsp. butter and the sour cream along with 1 cup sauce. Serve topped with remaining sauce.

STEAMED MUSSELS IN WINE BROTH

3 lbs. mussels
1 C. dry white wine
1 tsp. minced parsley
1 tsp. minced shallots
1 stick butter
Dash of cayenne pepper

Wash the mussels thoroughly, discarding any with broken shells or open shell that won't close when squeezed by hand. Place mussels in a large pot or steamer. Add wine, parsley and shallots. Steam for approximately 5 minutes or until shells open. Separate mussels from broth, placing mussels in a serving dish. By cooking the liquor, reduce liquid to ¾ cup. Add butter and pepper to broth and pour over mussels. Serve with pasta.

Mussels Grilled on Pine Needles

3 lbs. mussels
Dried pine needles

I use a lobster pot that had holes in the bottom. If you don't have a lobster pot, you can use a disposable foil pan that you have poked holes into the bottom. Layer dried pine needles on the bottom. Wash mussels thoroughly, discarding any with broken shells or open shells that won't close when squeezed by hand. Debeard any growths. Spread mussels on top of the pine needles. If using a lobster pot, cover with lid. If using the foil pan, cover with aluminium foil.

Put the pot/pan on top of the outdoor grill. Cook for 10 minutes. Check to see if mussels are opened. If not, recover and cook until mussels are open. Serve with melted butter.

Paella

Paella in Spain

1 Tbsp. olive oil

4 pcs. dark meat chicken

½ C. chopped onion

1 clove garlic, minced

1 can chicken broth

½ tsp. pepper

1 tsp. salt

½ tsp. tarragon

¼ tsp. paprika

1 C. raw rice

1 16-oz. can tomatoes

¼ lb. each: Shrimp, peeled and deveined; Sausage, Link, German or Italian

Sea Scallops, sliced into medallions
½ tsp. saffron

In a large pot or Paella pan, brown chicken in oil. Set aside chicken pieces. In the same oil sauté onion and garlic. Add broth and all seasonings EXCEPT saffron. Bring to a boil. Add rice. Cook covered over medium heat until rice absorbs half of the liquid. Add tomatoes, chicken, and sausage. Simmer covered 20 minutes. Add shrimp and scallops and cook for another ten minutes, or until seafood is cooked. Stir in the saffron. Liquid might have to be adjusted periodically. Mixture should be moist but not soupy. Rice should be cooked thoroughly. If the rice is not cooked, adjust moisture and cook until the rice is soft. Before serving, make sure chicken is cooked through.

An alternate method of cooking the chicken would be to grill the pieces and set aside until ready to add to the mixture.

Ceiling at Sangrada Familia, Barcelona, Spain

Desserts

Sacher Torte

¾ C. butter, softened

¾ C. sugar

7 oz, semisweet chocolate

8 egg yolks

1 C. all-purpose flour

10 egg whites

1 10-oz. jar apricot jam

Sacher Frosting

Sweetened whipped cream

Sacher Torte Frosting

4 oz. semisweet chocolate

4 oz. unsweetened chocolate

¼ C. butter

4 tsp. honey

Using a beater, cream butter with sugar until light and fluffy. Melt chocolate over hot water in a double boiler and beat into butter mixture. Beat in egg yolks, one at a time. In 3 batches, sift flour over mixture and gently fold in until just combined. DO NOT OVERMIX. Beat egg whites until stiff peaks form. Fold into batter. Again, DO NOT OVERMIX. Pour batter into greased and floured 9-inch springform pan. Bake in pre-heated 300-degree oven 50 to 60 minutes or until cake tests done with a toothpick. Remove from oven and cool 10 minutes on a cake rack. Remove from pan and continue cooling on rack.

Split the layer in half horizontally using a log sharp knife. Take 4 strips of wax paper and arrange in a square on the serving plate. Place the bottom layer on the serving plate with the wax paper half under the layer and half extended beyond the edges. Warm apricot jam and spread over top and sides of the bottom layer. Place top layer on top and spread apricot jam on top and sides of all. Let the apricot jam cool.

In the top of a double boiler over hot water, melt chocolate, butter, and honey, stirring until smooth. Let cool slightly. Reserve 2 tablespoons of frosting for creation of the writing on top. Pour warm frosting over cake using a spatula to encourage the frosting over the sides. You can tilt the cake slightly to cover sides. Let cool completely. Cool the reserved frosting in the refrigerator just until it becomes slightly harder. Fit a pastry bag with a small round pastry tip. Fill pastry bag with reserved chocolate. Write "Sacher" on the top of the cake with chocolate in the pastry bag. If you don't have a pastry bag, you can use an envelope or a plastic sandwich bag with a one corner snipped off.

After all the icing has hardened, gently remove the wax paper strips. Serve each piece with a dollop of the whipped cream.

Mini Pecan Tarts

Mini cupcake/tart pan
½ C. butter
3 oz. cream cheese
1 C. flour

Filling:
1 egg
1 tsp. melted butter
2/3 C. pecans, chopped
¾ C. light brown sugar
1 tsp. vanilla
¼ tsp. salt

Shells: Soften butter and cream cheese. Mix in flour. Kneed dough until just mixed. Roll in a ball; chill. Make smaller portions of dough for individual tarts. Break off a piece of dough about the size of a walnut. Flatten dough portion on a flat surface and then put into tart cups. Press dough against the bottom and sides.

Filling: Mix together all ingredients. Fill shells ½ full. Bake at 325° for 25-30 minutes or until shell is light brown.

Mamool: Lebanese Cookies

1 C. butter, softened

1 egg

½ C. sugar

¼ C. Farina (uncooked cream of wheat)

2 ½ C. flour

1 Tbsp. orange water

Beat first 3 ingredients until fluffy. Add remaining ingredients. Mix until dough ball forms. Chill dough.

Pecan Filling:

1 C. pecans

½ C. granulated sugar

1 Tbsp. orange water

Grind mixture on "pulse" in food processor. Mixture should be coarse.

Break pieces of dough off the size of a golf ball. Flatten with the palm of your hand or on a floured board. Press flattened dough into decorative mold that has been slightly floured.

Edges should extend out of the mold. Fill cavity with pecan mixture. Fold edges together and press to close over pecan mixture. Rap mold on cutting board to unmold. Place each piece on cookie sheet. Bake 10 to 15 minutes at 350° or until edges become slightly brown. Let cool. Dust with powdered sugar.

Wooden Mamool Molds
– Find at a Mediterranean food store

Flour cavity of mold, place flattened dough in the mold and fill with nut mixture.

Pinch together edges and unmold by tapping on cutting board.

BAKLAVA

1½ C. butter, clarified (already clarified butter can be bought at an import store. It is called Gee.)
3 cups Pecans or Pistachios, chopped
1 box of Phyllo Dough, thawed
2 cups Sugar
1 Tbsp. Orange Flower Water (can be obtained at Mediterranean grocery store)
½ C. Water
Parchment-lined shallow baking sheet

Unfurl Phyllo Dough. Separate first 3 sheets and lay on work surface. Using a soft pastry brush, brush with butter. Spread one line of crushed nuts one inch from the narrow end of phyllo. Roll up phyllo starting with the nut fill end. Place on baking sheet. Repeat until all phyllo is used. Paint all rolls with more butter. Cut 1-inch-long pieces on the diagonal. Bake 350° for 45 min. or until golden brown. Let cool before pouring syrup on top.

To make syrup, combine sugar, orange flower water and water in a saucepan. Boil until all of the sugar is dissolved. Pour over Baklava. Let cool. Baklava is ready to serve. Can be stored in covered container for 3 or 4 weeks (if it lasts that long).

This is how the Baklava looks when using the method that is described in my recipe.

This is the result of layering the Phyllo dough instead of rolling. Lay the dough flat in your baking pan 2 sheets at a time. Brush with the butter after each layer is laid down. When half the dough is in the pan, spread nut filling. Then repeat the layering of the Phyllo on top. Score in diamond pattern, cutting almost but not all the way through. Bake, cool and pour syrup over all as described in above recipe.

Applesauce Cake

3 C. all-purpose flour
2 tsp. baking soda
1 tsp. cinnamon
2 tsp. cloves
1 tsp. nutmeg
1 ½ C. pecan pieces
2 C. raisins
1 C. butter, softened
3 C. packed brown sugar
3 whole eggs
2 C. applesauce

Grease and flour generously large Bundt pan. Sift flour with dry ingredients. Dredge nuts and raisins in ¼-C. flour mixture to coat. Cream butter and sugar in large bowl. Add eggs and applesauce, then flour mixture.

Beat after each addition. Stir in nuts and raisins. Pour into pan. Bake in preheated 350° oven for 1 hour 15 min. Test for doneness.

The Beshara family did not like fruitcake for Christmas. Grandma Olga got this recipe from a neighbor. It became our family tradition for Christmas.

BLUEBERRY CRISP

9" square baking dish, buttered

3 C. blueberries, fresh or frozen

1 tsp. lemon juice

½ C. sugar

1/3 C. flour

1 tsp. cinnamon

¼ tsp. ginger

2 Tbsp. butter, melted

Gently mix berries with the lemon juice. Spread berries in a 9" square buttered baking dish. In a medium bowl mix sugar, flour, cinnamon and ginger. Add the butter and toss with a fork until mixture is crumbly. Sprinkle over berries.

Preheat oven 400°. Put berries in oven and bake 20 to 25 minutes or until topping is lightly brown. Cool about 10 minutes. Serve over ice cream.

Street Sculpture, Monte Carlo, Monaco

Candied Orange and Grapefruit Peel

2 large pink grapefruits

3 large oranges

3 ½ C. granulated sugar (divided use)

2 ¼ C. water, plus extra for boiling peels

Divide the peel of each grapefruit and orange into 4 segments by inserting a sharp knife and cutting only as deep as the peel. Carefully remove the peel, including the white pith, in 4 pieces. Save the fruit for another use. Cut each quarter into 8 or 9 lengthwise strips.

Place the peels in a large saucepan and cover with water. Bring to a boil and cook over moderate heat for 8 to 10 min. Drain. Repeat this step twice more to remove any bitterness in the peels. After the third time, drain and set the peels aside.

Add 3 cups of sugar to 2 ¼ C. of water in a large saucepan. Bring to a boil, stirring to dissolve the sugar. Add the strips of peel and simmer over low heat, stirring occasionally, until nearly all the syrup is absorbed, about 45 minutes.

With tongs, transfer the strips to a wire rack or a sheet of wax paper sprayed with non-stick cooking spray and let cool for at least 3 hours.

Place remaining ½ C. of sugar in a paper bag. Add the peel and gently toss. Remove from bag and shake off excess. Makes about 70 grapefruit peel strips and 90 orange peel strips.

If determined that the peels needed more drying at this stage, leave them out until they acquired a dry chewy consistency. Candied peel strips can be stored in an airtight container, wax paper between each layer, in a cool place for as long 3 months.

Orange Glazed Pecans with Leftover Syrup
Pour 2 cups of whole pecans into the remaining syrup. Stir to coat thoroughly. Spread pecans onto a cookie sheet lined with wax paper. Let cool.

Store in an airtight container.

Cannoli Shells

1 ¾ C. regular all-purpose flour

½ tsp. salt

2 Tbsp. granulated sugar

1 egg, slightly beaten

2 Tbsp. firm butter, cut in small pieces

¼ C. dry white wine

Oil for deep frying

Ricotta Filling (recipe to follow)

Powdered sugar

4 Cannoli tubular forms

Sift flour with salt and granulated sugar. Make a well in the center of the mixture and place egg and butter in well. Stir with a fork, working from center out to moisten flour mixture. Add wine, 1 Tbsp. at a time until dough begins to cling together. Use your hands to form dough into a ball. Cover and let stand for 15 min.

Roll dough out on floured board to about 1/16-inch thick. Cut into 3 1/2-inch circles. With a rolling pin, roll circles into ovals. Wrap dough circles around Cannoli Forms, sealing edges with egg white.

Pour oil in a deep fat fryer or electric skillet deep enough so the cannoli shells don't touch the bottom. Heat to 350°. CAREFULLY, as to not splash oil out of the pot, insert cannoli tubes into the oil. Fry 2 or 3 at a time for about 1 minute, turning once to evenly brown. Remove each with tongs to a paper towel-lined plate to drain. Let cool until you can touch the cannoli and tube. Be very careful! THEY ARE HOT! Slip the cannoli off the form. Repeat this step until shells are all cooked. Cool shells completely.

Sift powdered sugar over all shells. Makes 25. Shells can be stored in a covered container for a week or so.

Use a pastry tube to fill the shells with your choice of the following fillings. Fill just before serving.

Fillings

Ricotta Filling: Whirl 2 lbs. ricotta cheese in a blender or food processor until very smooth. Fold in 1 ½ C. unsifted powdered sugar and 4 tsp. vanilla. Add ¼ C. mini chocolate chips.

Amaretto Filling: Substitute Amaretto for the vanilla. Continue to use the chocolate chips.

Fluffy Ricotta Filling: Prepare ½ recipe Ricotta Filling, then fold in 1 cup heavy cream which has been whipped until stiff.

Pistachio Filling: To either of the above plain filling recipes fold in ¼ C. chopped pistachios.

Crème Brule

4 to 6 ramekins
1 C. heavy cream, divided
1 C. milk
1 C. granulated sugar
½ tsp. vanilla
5 egg yolks

Mix ¼ C. heavy cream with egg yolks. Bring the rest of cream, milk, sugar & vanilla to a boil. Cook and stir over medium heat until mixture is thick enough to coat the back of a spoon. Remove from heat and allow to steep. Allow to cool for a few minutes. Pour over cream/yolk mixture and mix well with a whisk. Place ramekins in a pan of water and bake 300° for 40 minutes. Remove from oven. Remove ramekins from the water and let cool. Sprinkle each with 2 Tbsp. sugar. I use a kitchen torch to melt the sugar to make a crust. If you don't have a torch, put ramekins in the oven and broil until the sugar has made a crust.

Refrigerate crème brule before serving.

I learned how to make this dish on a Mediterranean cruise. Good times!

Hershey Bar Cake

Bundt pan or tube pan

1 10-oz. milk chocolate Hershey Bar

1 C. butter, softened

2 C. sugar

4 eggs

1 C. buttermilk

½ tsp. salt

½ tsp. baking soda

2 ½ C. cake flour, sifted

1 5 ½-oz. can Hershey chocolate syrup

1 tsp. vanilla

Powdered sugar for topping

Melt bar in a double boiler or carefully in the microwave. With a mixer, cream butter and sugar. Beat in melted chocolate. Add eggs one at a time. Beat after each. Mix baking soda with salt and flour. Portion dry ingredients and buttermilk in half. Into the batter, add flour mixture and buttermilk, alternating dry and wet until all the buttermilk and flour is incorporated. Add chocolate syrup and vanilla and beat for one minute.

Pour batter into a greased and floured Bundt or tube pan.

Bake for 70 minutes at 350° or until toothpick comes out clean. Cool. Unmold onto a serving plate and sprinkle with powdered sugar. Serve with whipped cream.

LIGHT CHOCOLATE CAKE
("Light" meaning not dark chocolate)

1½ C. sugar

½ C. butter

2 oz. baking chocolate, melted

1 C. buttermilk

2 C. cake flour, sifted

2 whole eggs, slightly beaten

1 tsp. vanilla

½ tsp. salt

1 Tbsp. cider vinegar

1 tsp. baking soda

Grease and flour 3 8"-round cake pans. Cream sugar and butter together in a large mixing bowl until fluffy. Beat in 2 Tbsp. of the flour and all of the chocolate. Add eggs, buttermilk, remaining cake flour, vanilla and salt.

Beat until smooth. Then add vinegar and soda, beating only enough to blend thoroughly. Pour into prepared pans and bake in preheated oven 30 minutes at 350° or until toothpick comes out clean. Cool layers. Unmold from pans and ice with your choice of icing.

Mom was talking to a lady in a laundromat in Muskogee, Oklahoma, when she and Dad were first married in 1946. The lady was a home economics teacher in Muskogee Public Schools. She gave Mom this recipe. It is a light chocolate cake and was Dad's favorite.

Linzer Torte

1 ½ C butter

1 ½ C. confectioners' sugar

1 egg

2 ¾ C. all-purpose flour

1/8 tsp. salt

1 Tbsp. cocoa

1 tsp. cinnamon

1 ½ C. ground hazelnuts

1 12-oz. jar raspberry jam

In the container of a large food processor, cream butter with sugar until blended. Beat in egg. Combine dry ingredients and nuts into butter mixture, beat until blended. Turn out dough into bowl.

Press half the dough into a greased 10-inch springform pan. Spread with raspberry jam to within 1 inch of the edge. Roll out 2/3 of remaining dough on a floured cutting board. Cut into strips ½-inch wide. I use a very long slender knife to pick up the strips and arrange in a lattice design on the top of the raspberry layer. With the palms of the hands, roll remaining dough into ½-inch balls and place them around the outside edge of the torte. Press the balls gently into place, flattening slightly to make a scalloped edge. Bake on bottom rack of a preheated 375° oven 35 to 40 minutes or until edges have separated from the sides and are slightly brown. Cool torte and release from the spring form pan. Transfer the torte to a serving plate. Sprinkle with powdered sugar.

Texas Sunset